Creative Chemistry Experiments

Chemistry Book for Beginners
Children's Science Experiment Books

What would it be like to be a chemist? What do chemists do? Let's find out by doing a few easy chemistry experiments at home!

Chemistry

Chemistry is the study of matter, of the things that make up this world. Chemists study what matter is made up of, what its properties are, and how different substances work together.

Professional chemist senior woman looking through the microscope

Two substances can combine to make a third substance! Sometimes you can make a chemical change in a substance by an action as simple as heating it up!

People spend years studying the principles of chemistry, and working in well-equipped laboratories, to try to understand the world around us better.

But you can start much more simply than that, right in your own kitchen! Try out these simple experiments, and see what it feels like to do the sorts of things that chemists do. This may help you decide whether you want to do more chemistry, in a more serious way, in the future.

But first...

Principles for home chemistry

Before you get started, here are some general rules to follow in your kitchen chemistry experiments:

- Get permission: Your parents or the grownups you live with need to approve of what you are up to.

Happy mother with son studying chemistry.

- **Prepare:** Check the list of ingredients for each experiment and make sure you have what you need. Clear a space on a table or kitchen counter, making sure all food and all stuff that other people in your house care about is safely out of the way.

- Be safe: If the experiment involves a chemical that could sting if it gets on your skin, have a way to wash your hands quickly. If there is heat or an open flame involved, have a grownup standing by to help if things get out of control.

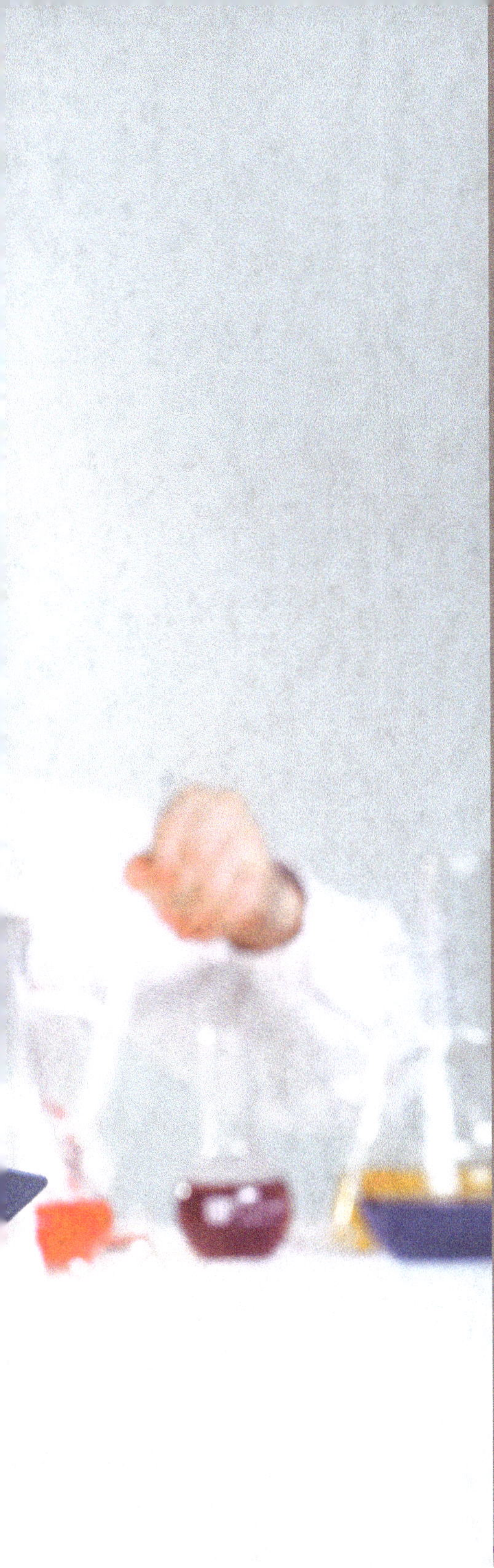

- **Take notes:** Somebody once said that taking notes turns goofing around into science! Record what you did, what you thought would happen, and what actually happened.

- Clean up after: Good scientists leave their labs in as good shape as they find them. If you want to be able to use your kitchen for chemistry a second time, you had better leave it neat and cleaned up after you are done with your first experiments. Don't leave a mess for somebody else.

Make borax snowflakes

Real snowflakes are made of frozen water and little bits of dust, and they fall from the sky in the winter. Borax snowflakes can happen in your kitchen!

What you need:

- String
- A jar with a wide mouth
- A pipe cleaner
- Borax (A mineral, also known as sodium borate, that you can find in some laundry detergents)
- A pencil
- Boiling water (get a grownup to help)
- Scissors
- Food coloring, if you want to add color to your snowflakes

1. Figure out how much water your jar can hold. Write down the amount.

2. Cut a pipe cleaner into three sections. Twist the sections together at their middle so you have a star with six arms. Trim the arms if you have to so the star fits into your jar.

Pipe cleaner

Jar

3. Tie one end of your string to one snowflake arm. Tie the other end around the pencil, with the string short enough so that if you balance the pencil on the jar mouth, the pipe cleaner star will hang in the jar without touching the side or the bottom. Take the star out of the jar.

4. Put the jar where it it can stay overnight without people messing with it.

5. Carefully pour boiling water into the jar so it will covers the pipe cleaner star.

6. For every cup of water the jar can hold, add three tablespoons of borax. Stir the water after every three tablespoons.

7. If you want, add a few drops of food coloring.

Boiling water

Borax crystals

8. Lower the pipe-cleaner star into the jar until the pencil is resting on the jar mouth and the pipe cleaners are covered with liquid. Leave the jar alone overnight.

9. In the morning, you will probably see that borax crystals have formed along the pipe cleaners, making a long-lasting snowflake shape. You can pick up the snowflake using the pencil, and hang it by its string to make a decoration.

What happened:

The combination of heat and liquid let the borax crystals form into a complicated, jagged shape.

Make a density column

Different substances have different densities, with water having a density of 1 gram per cubic centimeter (1g/cm3). Lead has a much higher density than that, so if you put lead in water, the lead will sink. Frozen water, or ice, floats because its density is less than that of liquid water.

You can make a colorful "stack" of household liquids of different densities, all in a single clear container!

Vase

- A clear container that is taller than it is wide. A large jar or a vase would be very good.

- A spoon

- Some of each of these liquids:
  1. Pancake syrup or maple syrup
  2. Liquid dish-washing soap
  3. Water with a few drops of food coloring
  4. Vegetable oil
  5. Rubbing alcohol with a few drops of a different color of food coloring
  6. Lamp oil

1. Put the container where you can easily pour things into it, but where it will not be in the way. See if you can put it where some sunlight can shine through it. Avoid bumping the container.

2. The liquids are numbered in the order you should use them. Take the first one and carefully pour some into the container to make a layer at the bottom. Try to keep the syrup from hitting the walls of the container, because that can make a messy result. One way to pour neatly is to put the spoon into the container, above whatever liquid is already there, and pour the next liquid so it hits the back of the spoon before it falls further.

Maple syrup

3. Add enough of each liquid to form a new layer in the density column. Be sure to add a good layer of vegetable oil before you add the alcohol layer, because if the alcohol can find a way through the oil layer, it will happily mix with the water layer. If you go slowly, these three layers should work fine.

4. Enjoy the display for a few days. Watch to see which liquids start to mix with their neighbors.

Density is just one element that controls whether liquids will mix with each other. Some liquids resist mixing together for other reasons: oil does not mix well with water, for instance.

Water and oil

Explore the properties of metal

With some pennies and some simple ingredients, you can understand more about metals.

Pennies

Dull penny

- Some old, dull pennies
- ¼ quarter cup of white vinegar, which has acetic acid
- One teaspoon of salt
- One clear glass or plastic bowl
- Water
- One mixing spoon
- Measuring spoons
- A paper towel
- A pen

What you do:

1. Put the vinegar and salt in the bowl together, and stir them to dissolve the salt into it.
2. Hold one penny halfway in the liquid for a few seconds. Then lift the penny out. What do you see? The half of the penny that was in the liquid is now clean!

vinegar and salt

Vinegar and salt mixture

3. Put the other pennies in the liquid and leave them there for five minutes. For the first minute things will be pretty active in the bowl!

Pennies get dull because the oxygen in the air has a reaction with the copper in the pennies and forms copper oxide, which is dark in color. The solution of salt and vinegar can dissolve the copper oxide, making the pennies look brand new again. The copper oxide leaves the pennies and stays in the liquid.

Paper towel

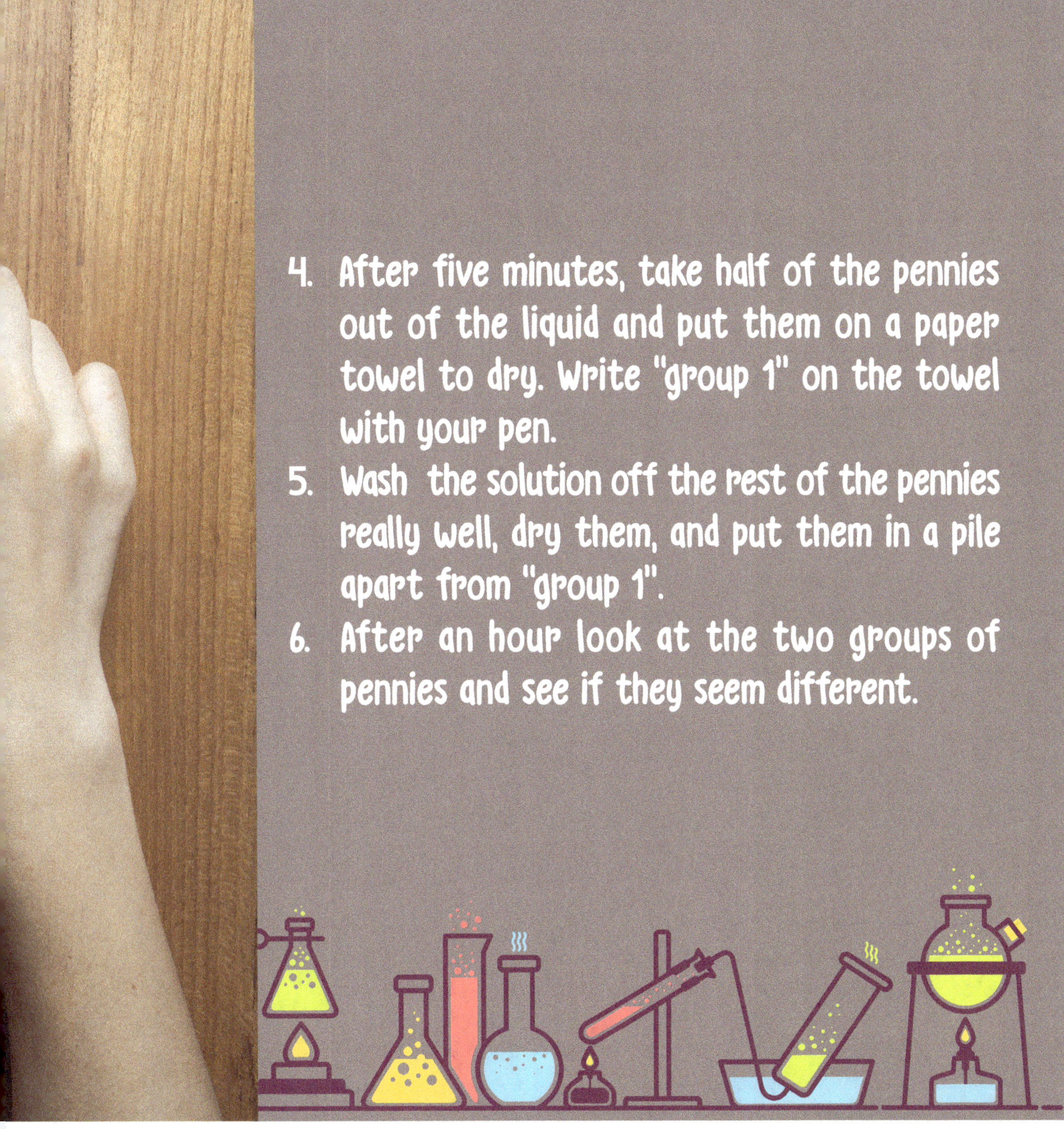

4. After five minutes, take half of the pennies out of the liquid and put them on a paper towel to dry. Write "group 1" on the towel with your pen.
5. Wash the solution off the rest of the pennies really well, dry them, and put them in a pile apart from "group 1".
6. After an hour look at the two groups of pennies and see if they seem different.

When you washed the solution off the second bunch of pennies, you stopped the reaction between the solution and the copper oxide. The pennies will stay new-looking for a while, and then slowly will get dull.

However, on the "group 1" pennies a different reaction starts! The acidic remnant on the pennies causes a reaction between the copper in the pennies and the oxygen in the air, and the coins will slowly turn a greenish color.

If you want clean pennies, it's good to know when to stop the reaction!

Science shows you the world

Small experiments can show you how larger experiments might go. You will get chances to do more chemistry in school, but you might also consider becoming a chemist and working in a lab when you grow up.

sin α
cos b
ab
S = ah = a² sin φ = Physics
= $\frac{d_1 \cdot d_2}{2}$
chemistry
HN
R
$t = 0.5$ mi
$S = h - 12$
$F = 3$ OH
$g = 1$
N
P

Other Baby Professor books, like Insects and Arachnids and Rocks and What We Know About Them – Geology for Kids, can show you other science areas you might like to study.

Visit
BABY PROFESSOR
EDUCATION KIDS
www.BabyProfessorBooks.com
to download Free Baby Professor eBooks
and view our catalog of new and exciting
Children's Books